Leptin Diet Cookbook

The Belly Fat Burnin' Recipe Book For Losing Weight FAST With The Leptin Diet

© **Copyright 2015 - All rights reserved.**

This document is geared towards providing exact and reliable information in regards to the topic and issue covered. The publication is sold with the idea that the publisher is not required to render accounting, officially permitted, or otherwise, qualified services. If advice is necessary, legal or professional, a practiced individual in the profession should be ordered.

- From a Declaration of Principles which was accepted and approved equally by a Committee of the American Bar Association and a Committee of Publishers and Associations.

In no way is it legal to reproduce, duplicate, or transmit any part of this document in either electronic means or in printed format. Recording of this publication is strictly prohibited and any storage of this document is not allowed unless with written permission from the publisher. All rights reserved.

The information provided herein is stated to be truthful and consistent, in that any liability, in terms of inattention or otherwise, by any usage or abuse of any policies, processes, or directions contained within is the solitary and utter responsibility of the recipient reader. Under no circumstances will any legal responsibility or blame be held against the publisher for any reparation, damages, or monetary loss due to the information herein, either directly or indirectly.

Respective authors own all copyrights not held by the publisher.

The information herein is offered for informational purposes solely, and is universal as so. The presentation of the information is without contract or any type of guarantee assurance.

The trademarks that are used are without any consent, and the publication of the trademark is without permission or backing by the trademark owner. All trademarks and brands within this book are for clarifying purposes only and are the owned by the owners themselves, not affiliated with this document.

Table of Contents

Introduction 4
Chapter 1: Leptin Diet And Weight Loss 5
Chapter 2: Recommended Breakfast Recipes 10
Chapter 3: Recommended Main Dish Recipes 17
Chapter 4: Recommended Snacks And Side Dishes 24
Chapter 5: 7 Day Meal Plan 28
Free preview of : *"Ketogenic Diet Cookbook"* 32

Introduction

I want to thank you and congratulate you for purchasing the book, *"Leptin Diet: The Belly Fat Burnin' Recipe Book For Losing Weight FAST With The Leptin Diet".*

This book contains proven steps and strategies on how you can lose weigh fast and naturally by increasing the Leptin levels in your body and taking advantage of its effects. Among its many benefits would be a boost in our body's ability to metabolize food, providing us with stable energy levels throughout the day and preventing the body from storing fat.

If you're dieting, remember that it would always be in your favor to work with your body's natural mechanisms instead of working against it. With the Leptin diet, you'll be able to achieve your weight goals without having to starve yourself in the process.

Thanks again for purchasing this book, I hope you enjoy it!

Chapter 1: Leptin Diet And Weight Loss

These days, the mere mention of a new diet often draws suspicious and questioning looks from most people. Unsurprisingly, of course, as there has been many a scam diet that's cropped up in the past years. Numerous weight loss pills and drinks have been marketed to be totally effective only to turn out bogus or even dangerous to one's health. So what makes the Leptin Diet different? Well, to begin with, it isn't one of those unorthodox fad diets or a supplement that you take before every meal. To put it simply, it is a smarter and healthier way of looking at the food you consume- it isn't about how much you eat, it's all about **when** you are eating it.

Time isn't usually a factor when it comes to most diets. After all, who pays attention to the hour that they eat? For most folks, losing weight means eating much less than what they normally do. While this method works, there are also certain risks involved often seen in cases wherein a person begins to overdo the diet. Some refrain from even touching food at all. But what if there is a way to lose weight without having to go through the trouble of counting calories? Instead, you only need to be more mindful of what and when you consume. By having more awareness when it comes to these things, you can gain more control over your body as well as your overall weight loss.

Now, let's talk a bit more about the science of this particular diet. There is a little known 16-Da adipokine molecule called Leptin and by understanding it better, you increase your chances of losing weight faster but in a healthier way. After all, it is one of the major hormones that is responsible for managing the overall balance of our body.

So how exactly does it help with weight loss?

- Controls excessive fat storage. Our body stores fat for many different reasons and in most cases, it does this as a precaution- just in case you end up going for days without food. See, if you go on a starvation diet, this sets off a trigger in your body wherein instead of burning any fat you consume for energy, it begins storing it for future use. Leptin can help you control what is stored into fat and what is used for energy. You can make sure that your body uses more of the fat for fuel so that you don't end up with any excesses in the areas you don't want them in.

- Suppresses food cravings. Considered by many dieters as the foremost challenge when it comes to losing weight, cravings can certainly be hard to overcome. This is especially if you're just starting out with the process and have been used to indulging yourself whenever the craving appears. Did you know that there are cases wherein people have reportedly experienced extreme mood swings while dieting simply because they've been craving certain food but can't have it? You wouldn't want to reach that point so let Leptin make things easier for you. The hormone itself is capable of suppressing any cravings; acting as a mediator when it comes to long-term energy regulation thus lowering your desire for food. After all, we only begin to crave these things whenever the body feels like its low on fuel. So by properly regulating the energy flow, we can go on for longer without feeling the need to stuff ourselves full.

**People who suffer from obesity actually have this hormone too but it is in very short supply. This is why people with the disease often find themselves wanting to consume more and more food. They may also feel as if they have no control over their cravings and to some extent, this is true. The body reacts to its needs instinctively and the cravings can be hard to ignore. They consume far more food than their bodies truly need and because there's also a lack of proper energy regulation, they wind up feeling lethargic and unable to exercise to burn off the excess fat.

With that said, it doesn't mean that they won't be able to lose the weight they have gained. Obesity is not a death sentence, regardless of the Leptin levels in their bodies. There are over the counter Leptin supplements available and couple that with proper discipline when it comes to eating better as well as exercising more, they too can begin to shed off the pounds.

5 Leptin Diet Rules:

Now that we've covered the basics of the diet itself, let's talk about a few simple guidelines that should help you stay on track when it comes to following it. The thing with the Leptin diet is that it is more of a lifestyle overhaul instead of a meal plan that you need to follow thoroughly. Whilst there is a meal plan involved and a few restrictions when it comes to what and when you eat, it still is more than just a simple diet. It all comes down to the dietary choices you make each day and how you can make better ones to improve your health. Shall we get started?

- **Do not eat after dinner.** For most people, having a midnight snack some hours after dinner actually helps them de-stress. In some cases, it can even help them sleep better. However, if you're trying to lose weight then this is something that you might want to try and avoid doing. Why? Eating after dinner, especially as the night gets later, can actually counteract any exercise or dieting that you're doing. The later in the evening you eat, the greater the chance that your body's simply going to store the food you consume as fats instead of using it as fuel. This is because during these hours, Leptin isn't working as well as it did during the day. To avoid this from happening, always eat at least 4 hours before your bedtime. This should give your body enough time to metabolize the food and prevent it from getting stored as fats. You can also choose to limit the amount of food you eat at night to make it easier for your body to digest.

- **Always eat three full meals a day.** How many times a day do you end up eating snacks? It's hard to keep track of, right? Did you know that eating small things in between your daily meals is actually one of the main reasons as to why people get sidetracked when it comes to their diets? This is because these are easy to lose track of and when you're rushing to and fro, you're not really giving much thought to what you're consuming- and its effects on your body. People think that by eating smaller things, they are also consuming less calories. So it doesn't really have any effect on the diet, right? Wrong. What you're developing is a habit that will surely derail your weight loss plans. Another thing that snacking does is decrease the amount of Leptin in your body. More often than not, people would snack on the things they can find easily. Beverages such as sodas and coffee can significantly lower Leptin levels in the body so avoid this at all costs. Try sticking to only 3 full meals a day and if you're unable to- snack only once or twice and choose something healthy to eat. You can also opt to drink water instead of eating something. It helps you feel fuller.

- **Avoid eating large meals.** Since you're eliminating snacks from your daily diet, you might find yourself compensating for this by eating large meals instead. Some people would assume that this is completely fine but the truth is that it actually does more harm than good. This is because your body can only use up a certain amount of the food you consume for energy and if there happens to be any excess, it will get stored as fat. Unless you plan on working out later in the day to burn off the extra calories, avoiding large meals is certainly a good idea. Larger meals can also affect the production of Leptin in your system and can actually lead to an increased resistance, making you feel hungrier even if you've already eaten a lot. This is one of the many "traps" that people fall into. Because less Leptin is produced, you'll find yourself eating more and more- regardless of the meal size.

- *Always have protein for breakfast*. For most people, dinner is the biggest meal of the day and many tend to skip breakfast completely. However, this is the one thing that you shouldn't do if you're trying to lose weight. If you want to boost Leptin levels in your body and make sure that you don't end up craving throughout most of the day, the biggest and most important meal should be breakfast. It is important for our bodies to get the fuel it needs during the morning. Not only will it help us get ready to face the day but it also gives us a great excuse to eat a large meal- knowing that we'll be able to burn it off as we work. For breakfast, proteins are really great to have as it can actually help in waking up our body systems. Protein is also great, lasting fuel so you wouldn't have to worry about running out of steam mid-morning.

- *Reduce the amount of carbs that you eat*. You don't have to completely eliminate it from your diet but it would certainly help your weight loss goals if you eat less of it. This is a little hard to do, however, considering many of your favorite foods are most likely part of the carbohydrate family. From sweet and delectable pastries, savory pastas and cheeses- who can say no to these things? Whilst they taste fantastic, however, they are actually no good if you're looking to lose excess pounds. The body chooses them out of survival instinct, one that we developed in the past when food was scarce and we needed to store as much fat as we can in order to thrive. This becomes problematic in this day and age, of course, since acquiring food is no longer an issue. So do limit your carb intake and choose only the best kind. This includes: vegetables, fruits, small amounts of butter, cottage cheese and yogurt. As much as possible, avoid grain and grain products when it comes to your daily diet.

Is it safe to exercise while doing the Leptin diet?

Given that there are certain dietary restrictions to the diet itself, this question is completely warranted. The answer, however, depends on a case-to-case basis. It is safe that if you're only performing simple exercises such as running or continuing a pre-existing exercise regimen then it should be okay. If you intend on starting a new one, talking to your trainer or physician beforehand would certainly help. Always remember that when you're on a diet, there are resources that your body might not be receiving since you're cutting out certain food items from your daily meals. Keep the balance between diet and exercise, this is the golden rule.

Chapter 2: Recommended Breakfast Recipes

When it comes to breakfasts, the diet recommends that you opt for a high protein one in order to raise Leptin levels in the body. Aside from this, there are many benefits to enjoying a high-protein breakfast everyday. Not only does it increase Leptin levels, it can also boost your metabolism and gives you more energy to get you through the day. The more energy you can produce the better your metabolism becomes and the more calories you get to burn. Great, huh?

There is only one con to a high protein breakfast and that would be the fact that preparing it can eat up a lot of time. Who would want to prepare meat or fish first thing in the morning? If you're always in a rush and don't have the luxury of preparing a proper breakfast meal, opt for simple yet protein rich smoothies. There are countless recipes that are no only filling but would also provide you with the protein you need for that day.

To help you get started, here are some recipes that you might want to try:

- **Egg White Frittata**

Ingredients: 1 red pepper (chopped), 1 green pepper (chopped), 2 tablespoons of olive oil, 1 teaspoon kosher salt, ¼ of a yellow onion (chopped), 1 teaspoon of black pepper, ½ cup of feta cheese (crumbled), 8 egg whites (separated) and 2 cups of fresh spinach.

Directions:

- Preheat your oven to 375
- Take a skillet and add some olive oil to it, bring this to medium-low heat
- Saute your peppers and onions until both become tender. This should take no more than 7 minutes.
- Sprinkle some salt and pepper to this mixture.
- Add your egg whites to the skillet and cook it for another 3 minutes.
- Sprinkle some spinach and feta cheese on top.

- Put everything in the oven and bake it for about 10 minutes. If you're using whole eggs instead of just whites, make sure you bake it at 400.
- Serve warm.

- **Low Carb Hotcakes**

Ingredients: 1 tablespoon of ground of flaxseed, 3 cups of almond meal, ½ a teaspoon of baking soda, ½ teaspoon of sea salt, 3 eggs, 2/4 cup of unsweetened almond milk (you can also use coconut milk or plain milk), and 2 tablespoons of extra-light olive oil (coconut oil and walnut oil can also be used).

Directions:

- Get a medium bowl and in it, combine your baking soda, salt, flaxseed and almond meal.
- Next, get a larger bowl and whisk your eggs in it. Add the milk as well as your oil (or better, depending on what you're using) and whisk everything thoroughly.
- Carefully mix the flour mixture with your egg mixture, whisking gently as you pour. Add more milk if you find it necessary. The mixture's consistency should be similar to that of pancake batter.
- Lightly oil your skillet and place this over medium heat. Pour about ¼ of your batter onto it and cook for 3 minutes. Check for bubbles or if the edges are cooked before flipping it over. Cook the other side for another 3 minutes then set aside. Repeat the same process for the rest of the mixture.
- You can serve this with fresh Greek yogurt, fresh fruit or even your favorite maple syrup to naturally sweeten your meal.

- **Turkey Sausage Muffin**

Ingredients (Sausage): ½ a medium onion (finely chopped), 1 tablespoon of olive oil, ½ a pound of ground turkey, 1 clove of garlic (minced), 1 teaspoon of dried oregano (crumbled), 1 teaspoon of fennel seeds, ½ a teaspoon of ground black pepper, 1 teaspoon of dried basil, 1 teaspoon dried parsley and ½ a teaspoon of sea salt.

Ingredients (Muffins): 2 cups of finely chopped broccoli, ½ cup of sun-dried tomatoes, 1 cup of shredded cheddar, ½ teaspoon of dried oregano, 1 teaspoon of dried basil, ½ a teaspoon of onion powder, ½ a teaspoon of sea salt, 8 large eggs and 1 tablespoon of chives.

Directions:

- Preheat your oven to 350. After, grease a muffin pan- preferably one that fits 12 all at once.
- Using a medium sized skillet over low heat, cook your garlic and onion for at least 5 minutes or up until the onion softens. Remove from the heat and let it cool for 10 minutes. Set aside.
- In a bowl, combine your onion mixture with the turkey. Add the rest of your ingredients into this and make sure that everything is incorporated properly.
- Form patties following your preferred thickness. Cook each over medium heat for about 8 minutes or until the meat turns from pink to golden brown. Set this aside and allow to cool before crumbling it up into bite sized pieces.
- Next, mix your sausage, broccoli, tomatoes, cheese, oregano, basil, salt and onion powder together.
- Whisk the eggs thoroughly and pour it into the broccoli mixture. Blend well and divide it evenly among the muffin cups. Top this with some chives.
- Bake for at least 30 minutes and allow to cool down before serving.

- **Baked Eggs In Ham Cups**

Ingredients: 12 slices of ham, 12 eggs, pepper, salt and paprika.

Directions:

- Preheat your oven to 375.
- Line a muffin thin with the slices of ham. Gently crack an egg into each spot then evenly season with salt, pepper and paprika.
- Bake this for about 20 minutes and allow to cool for another 3 before serving.

- **Quinoa Egg Bake**

Ingredients: 1 teaspoon of butter or any substitute that you prefer, 8 eggs, ½ cup of uncooked quinoa, 1 tablespoon of garlic (chopped), 1 ¼ cup of nonfat milk, 1 teaspoon of thyme (chopped), ½ teaspoon of salt, ½ teaspoon of pepper, 2 cups of baby spinach (roughly chopped) and a cup of finely shredded parmesan or romano cheese.

Directions:

- Preheat your oven to 350. Take a baking dish and grease it with some butter.
- Place your quinoa into a strainer and rinse it under cold water until it runs clear. Make sure that you drain it well.
- Take a large bowl and whisk your milk, eggs, thyme, garlic, pepper, salt and quinoa together. Stir in your spinach and make sure everything is evenly coated before transferring it to the baking dish.
- Cover this tightly with some foil and tap gently to make sure that the quinoa sets evenly at the bottom. Bake until it sets- this should take about 45 minutes.
- Remove the foil and sprinkle the top with some cheese. Place it back in the oven and let it bake uncovered for some 15 minutes more or until the ham goes golden, crisp.
- Set aside and allow to cool before serving.

- **Tomato Frittata**

Ingredients: 4 ripe tomatoes, 4 eggs, 2 pieces of bacon (fried and diced), 1 tablespoon of ghee, salt and pepper for seasoning.

Directions:

- Preheat your oven to 425.
- Cut the tops of the tomatoes and using a spoon, gently clean out the inside.
- Next, evenly divide your diced bacon between the 4 tomatoes. Scramble the four eggs and pour an equal amount of it into each tomato bowl. Layer it on top of the bacon.
- Evenly divide the ghee between your 4 uncooked eggs and place one on top of each tomato. Sprinkle with some salt and pepper.
- Bake for about 40 to 50 minutes depending on how fast the eggs are cooked through. Eat warm.

- **Kale And Banana Power Breakfast Smoothie**

Ingredients: 1 ripe banana, 1/3 cup of strawberries, 1/3 cup of blueberries, ½ a cup of kale leaves, 1 tablespoon of ground flax seeds, ¼ cup of almond milk (you can also use water), 1 tablespoon of hemp powder, 1 tablespoon of acai, 1 tablespoon of chia seeds and 1 teaspoon of cinnamon.

Directions:

- Blend all of your ingredients, adding as much liquid as you prefer into the mix. For something thicker, less milk is best. However, if you want something lighter then add a bit more of it.
- To add a bit of texture, add some chia or hemp seeds as toppings.

- **Coconut And Almond Protein Shake**

Ingredients (Nuts): ¼ cup of unsweetened shredded dried coconut, ¾ cup of raw almonds and 2 cups of warm water.

Ingredients (Shake): 2 cups of cold water, 1 scoop of vanilla protein powder, 1 teaspoon of kosher or celtic sea salt, 2 teaspoons of grated ginger, 1 teaspoon of vanilla extra, 1 teaspoon of ground cinnamon, 2 tablespoons of coconut butter and honey.

Directions:

- The night before: combine your almonds, coconuts, salt and 2 cups of water in one container. Make sure all of the nuts are covered in water. Let this sit for about 8 hours. Doing this should help activate the nuts as well as break down the phytic acid in them which can cause bloating. Soaking also makes them much easier for the body to digest.

- In the morning: Drain the almonds and coconut water then add both to a blender. To this, add 2 cups of cold filtered water, protein powder, cinnamon, ginger, vanilla and the coconut butter. Blend until it becomes smooth.

- If you want a thinner shake, pass the mixture through a sieve. This should remove any of the additional fibers.

- Sweeten according to your taste.

- **Coffee and Banana Smoothie**

Ingredients: 1 cup chilled brewed coffee, 1 cup nonfat plain Green yogurt, 1 ½ bananas (cut into small chunks), 1 tablespoon ground flax seed, ½ teaspoon ground cinnamon, 2 teaspoons of agave nectar or honey, ¼ teaspoon of grated nutmeg and 6 ice cubes.

Directions:

- Place all of your ingredients in a blender. Do make sure that it is capable of crushing ice.

- Blend until smooth.

**When it comes to breakfast smoothies, the fun is in experimenting with

different combinations! Hardly anyone can go wrong with this so try out different ingredients and who knows? You might discover your favorite this way.

Chapter 3: Recommended Main Dish Recipes

When it comes to your main dishes, it needs to be properly balanced and filling. Of course, flavor is a major factor here too so you actually get to enjoy the meal itself. What you have for lunch can be the same thing you'll for dinner too but if you're conscious of what you consume later in the day- something lighter would certainly work best. Now, we all know that thinking about what to make for yourself or your family on a daily basis can be quite the frustrating experience. To help you out, here are a few easy and health recipes that you can try out.

- **Chicken Cutlets With Cherry Salsa**

Ingredients: ½ a pound of cherries (pitted), ¾ teaspoon salt, ½ a cup of chopped white onion, 1 large ripe cherry tomato (roughly chopped), ½ a teaspoon of ground black pepper, ¾ cup of whole wheat breadcrumbs, 2 tablespoons of fresh cilantro, 4 boneless and skinless chicken cutlets and 2 tablespoons of extra virgin olive oil.

Directions:

- Combine your onion, cherries, tomato, salt and pepper into a food processor. Pulse until you end up with a chunky salsa. If you don't own a processor, finely chopping all of your ingredients would work just the same. Once done, stir in the cilantro and set everything aside.
- Take your breadcrumbs and place them into a wide dish. Season your chicken with ½ a teaspoon of salt and ¼ teaspoon of pepper before dredging it in breadcrumbs. Make sure that you coat the whole piece evenly before transferring it to a new plate.
- Heat some oil on your skillet over medium heat. Cook your chicken thoroughly and until the skin turns golden brown. This should take about 6 to 8 minutes.
- Transfer to your plate and spoon some of the salsa on top or serve it on the side.

- **Coconut Rice And Grilled Shrimp**

Ingredients: 1 white onion, 2 tablespoons of olive oi, 6 cloves of garlic, 2 red peppers (diced), 2 roma tomatoes, 1 teaspoon of fresh ginger, ¼ cup of unsweetened coconut (grated), 1 ¾ cups of basmati rice, 3 cups of water, ½ cup chopped parsley, 1 cup of organic low fat vanilla yogurt, 1 lb of shrimp (deveined and peeled), salt and pepper to taste.

Directions:

- Heat some olive on a pan over medium heat. Add your peppers and onions to this. Cook for about 5 minutes or until the onion turns translucent.
- Stir in your ginger and garlic then cook until it becomes fragrant. To this, add your coconut and tomatoes. Cook for another 5 minutes.
- Add your rice to the mix and stir frequently until it becomes lightly browned. This should take about 2 minutes. Add some water and stir, making sure to combine both elements well. Bring this to a boil and reduce your heat. Cover and allow this to simmer for 20 minutes.
- Remove everything from the heat. Now, take a small bowl and temper the yogurt by adding some of the rice mixture to it. Mix well. Continue doing this until the yogurt becomes warmed through.
- Add some parsley , salt and pepper to taste. Fold everything together and combine well.
- For your shrimp, take some skewers and thread about 4 pieces in each. Grill this over medium heat for a minute or 2 per side. The shrimp should remain white in the center.

- **Chicken Chili**

Ingredients: 1 tablespoon of olive oil, 1 cup of onions (diced), 1 pound of organic chicken breast (cubed), 1 15 ounce can of organic white beans, 1 15 ounce can of stewed tomatoes, 2 cloves of garlic (minced), 1 fresh jalapeno, 2 tablespoons of chili powder, ¼ teaspoon of ground cumin, ½ teaspoon of dried oregano, salt and pepper to taste.

Directions:

- Take your skillet and coat it with some olive oil. Add your chicken and onions. Brown the chicken over medium heat until it cooks through.
- Add your other ingredients to this and continue cooking everything on low heat for at least another 15 minutes.
- If you want to increase spiciness, add some red pepper flakes or diced green chillies. Top with some cilantro before serving.

- **Healthy Turkey Burger**

Ingredients: 1 pound of organic ground turkey, ¼ cup of organic gouda cheese, 1 cup organic marinara sauce, ¼ cup organic mozzarella cheese, whole grain burger bun or pita wrap (depending on your preference), organic salad greens, ½ a cup of chopped red onion, salt and pepper to taste.

Directions:

- Mix all of your ingredients together with the ground turkey except for the onions, and the salad greens.
- From this mixture, make about 4 individual patties and bake this at 420 for about 15 minutes. You can also opt to use a grill.
- Once done, let it cool before topping it with the red onions and salad greens. Serve in a burger bun or a pita bread.

- **Poached Salmon With Mango Salsa**

Ingredients (Salsa): 1 cup of fresh or frozen mango cubes, ½ cup of red onions (diced), 1 Serrano chili, ¼ cup of cilantro (chopped) and the juice of ½ a lime.

Ingredients (Poached Salmon): 2 cups of dry white wine (you can also use fish stock), 2 cups of water, 6 peppercorns, 2 tablespoons of fresh dill weed, 1 sliced lemon, 1 celery stalk (chopped), 1 onion (sliced) and 6 wild Salmon fillets.

Directions:

- To make your salsa, combine your chili, cilantro, onion and lime together. Mix well. Season this with some salt and pepper then set aside.

- In a large skillet, combine your wine (or your fish stock), peppercorns, water, celery, dill, lemon and onion. Bring this to a boil then cover. Reduce your head and allow this to simmer for at least 10 minutes to blend the flavors together.

- Add the salmon to your skillet and allow to simmer for another 10 minutes or up until the fish becomes flakier.

- Plate the fillets and garnish with your salsa on the side or on top.

- **Steak Burritos**

Ingredients (Marinade): 2 jalapenos, ¾ cup olive oil, ¼ cup of cumin seeds, 1 teaspoon salt, 1 bunch of cilantro, 1 tablespoon cracked black pepper, ½ cup of lime juice and 1 clove of garlic.

Ingredients (Rice, steak and burrito): ½ a cup of prepared salsa, ¼ cup of uncooked long grain brown rice, ½ a cup of water, 1 15 ounce can of organic black beans, 1 tablespoon olive oil, 12 ounces of grass-fed strip steak, ½ a cup of shredded sharp cheddar cheese, 1 8 inch pieces of whole wheat tortillas, 2 tablespoons of coarsely chopped cilantro and ¼ cup of fresh guacamole.

Directions:

- Marinade: Combine all of your ingredients in a blender and mix this until it becomes smooth. Pour this over your beef slices. Cover and let it refrigerate overnight.

- Cook rice according to directions. When there's only about 10 minutes of cooking time left, add the salsa and water to your rice. Allow this to simmer for 5 minutes before stirring in the beans. Let this simmer again until the rice becomes tender and the liquid dissipates. This should take about 5 minutes or more.

- In a skillet, heat some oil over medium heat and add your steak slices to it.

Cook evenly.

- To serve, divide the steak among your tortillas and top this with equal amounts of guacamole, cheese, cilantro and your rice mixture. Roll carefully and serve.

- **Chicken Kebabs**

Ingredients: 3 tablespoons Tamari, the juice of 1 line, 1 tablespoon of extra virgin olive oil, 1 teaspoon minced garlic, 4 skinless boneless organic chicken and some cilantro to add flavor.

Directions:

- In a small bowl, mix your Tamari sauce, lime juice and extra virgin olive oil together. Add a bit of the chopped cilantro too as well as the garlic. Stir and set aside.

- Cut your chicken to large chunks and skewer them. Marinate these in the mixture for at least 30 minutes to an hour depending on the amount of time you have.

- Grill on medium high heat for about 8 minutes on each side or until the juices run clear. You can serve this with some steamed veggies or fresh salad.

- **Wild Salmon With Pepita Lime Butter**

Ingredients: 1 ½ pounds of uncooked wild salmon, 2 tablespoons of chili sauce, 3 tablespoons of Tamari sauce, 2 teaspoons of sesame oil, 2 tablespoons of olive oil, 2 teaspoons of rice wine, 3 cloves of garlic (minced), freshly cracked black pepper and 1 scallion (sliced thinly).

Directions:

- Begin by toasting the pepitas. After, place these in a small bowl together with the lime zest, butter, lime juice and chili powder.

- Take a large skillet and grease it with olive oil. Place this over medium heat. Before adding your salmon to it, sprinkle it with some salt and pepper. Cook this until browned which should take no more than 4 minutes for each side.

- Remove your pan from the heat and transfer your salmon to a different plate. Add your butter and lime mixture to the still hot plan. Stir this until the butter melts.

- Top the salmon with your butter sauce before serving.

- **Pesto Shrimp With Quinoa And Brussel Sprouts**

Ingredients: 1 pound fresh large shrimp, 2 cups of cooked quinoa, ½ a cup of fresh pesto, 1 lb brussel sprouts, 4 oz shitake mushrooms, 2 tablespoons of mustard seeds, salt and pepper to taste.

Directions:

- Devein the shrimp and peel them. Rinse before cooking. When cooking the shrimp, you can either steam or pan fry them, making sure not to cook them for too long as this could make them chewy. Once you're done cooking the shrimp, allow it too cool for a bit before mixing in the pesto. Make sure that everything is coated evenly.

- For the quinoa, boil about 2 cups of water and add a cup of the grain to it. Make sure your heat is at the lowest setting. Allow this to simmer- the process should take no more than 20 to 25 minutes.

- As for the brussel sprouts, cut off the bottoms and slice the heads in half. Your mushrooms should be sliced into long strips. Next, add these to a pan over medium heat. Mix in your mustard seeds and allow to cool for at least 5 minutes. Sprinkle some salt and pepper to taste.

- Serve in individual bowls. ½ a cup of the quinoa should be topped by at least 4 to 6 ounces of the pesto shrimp. Serve the brussel sprouts as a side dish.

*When it comes to your main meals, balance remains key. Only eat the amount

that you'll be able to burn throughout the day. Once dinner comes around, opt for something lighter. Some salad greens- anything that's easy to digest and metabolize. After all, your body no longer has any need for a lot of energy since you're preparing for rest.

Chapter 4: Recommended Snacks And Side Dishes

If you're looking to have a snack, better make a healthy choice. Instead of buying chips or ordering from a fast food, why not make your own and take it to wherever you're going? Not only is this the cheaper option, it also allows you make use of the freshest ingredients. To help you get started, below are some easy to make snacks as well as side dishes that's sure to tickle your palate.

- **Quinoa And Lentil Salad**

Ingredients: 1 cup of organic lentils, 1 cup of organic quinoa, 2 teaspoons of salt, 3 tablespoons of extra virgin olive oil, 3 tablespoons of balsamic vinegar, 1 plum tomato, 1 avocado, 2 tablespoons of lemon zest and 2 tablespoons of fresh cilantro.

Directions:

- Take the lentils and place these in a pot. Add enough water to cover them with at least 2 inches. Stir a tablespoon of salt and allow this to boil. Let it reduce to a simmer and cook for about 10 to 15 minutes or until it becomes tender.
- Cook the quinoa according to directions.
- Drain the lentils and mix it with the quinoa. Stir and make sure it combines well. Set aside and allow to cool.
- In a separate bowl, whisk together your olive oil and some vinegar. Add your avocado and tomato to the lentil mixture. Drizzle it with the vinaigrette.
- Top with lemon zest and cilantro before serving.

- **Crunchy Kale Salad**

Ingredients: 1 bunch of kale, 1/3 small sweet onion, ½ a cup of cooked chickpeas,

1/3 cups of raisins, ½ a cup of lemon juice, 1/3 cup of organic sesame tahini, a pinch of cayenne and a teaspoon of Himalayan salt.

Directions:

- Wash the kale and strip the ribs. Mix this together with the raisins, sliced onion and chickpeas.
- Whisk together the rest of your ingredients. If the tahini is too thick, add about a tablespoon or two of water then whisk again.
- Toss the leaves together with the mixture before serving.

- **Heirloom Tomato and Mozarella Salad**

Ingredients: 1 carton of fresh mozzarella, 1 carton of small heirloom tomatoes, 3 tablespoons of olive oil, fresh basil, 2 tablespoons of balsamic vinegar, salt and pepper to taste.

Directions:

- Mix the olive oil, balsamic vinegar, salt and pepper in a small bowl. Set aside.
- Combine your tomatoes, mozzarella and basil. Drizzle this with some of the dressing and toss before serving.

- **Kale Chips**

Ingredients: 1 bunch of kale, cold pressed extra virgin olive oil and some sea salt.

Directions:

- Preheat your oven to 350
- Wash the kale, drain the water then tear out the center stem. Tear up the leaves into 3 inch pieces. If you have a salad spinner, use it to further dry the leaves.
- Place it on a baking sheet, make sure nothing overlaps. Drizzle some olive

oil on each piece and massage to coat evenly. Lightly salt this.

- Bake until it gets crisp. After 5 minutes, turn the baking sheet and bake for another 3.
- Allow to cool before serving!

- **Fully Loaded Avocado**

Ingredients: 1 avocado, lemon wedge, ¼ cup of organic 2% cottage cheese, small organic tomato and some sea salt.

Directions:

- Carefully, cut your avocado in half and take out the pit.
- Fill the halves with cottage cheese then top it with some tomato.
- Squeeze some lemon juice on top and add a sprinkle of salt.

- **Healthy Yogurt Parfait**

Ingredients: 1 cup or organic plain yogurt, ¼ cup of organic goji berries, ¼ cup of organic raw granola and some organic honey for added sweetness.

Directions:

- Add some of your goji berries, granola and some of the honey to your yogurt. Mix everything well.
- Transfer this to a serving dish and top with the same, except for the honey.
- Best chilled before serving.

- **Chocolate Chili Smoothie**

Ingredients: 1 cup of 2% organic milk, 1 scoop of daily protein chocolate, ½ teaspoon of cinnamon, 1 teaspoon of honey, ¼ teaspoon of cayenne and 4 ice cubes.

Directions:

- Blend everything together until it becomes smooth. Adjust the sweetness using the honey.

** Remember, with snacks, moderation is important. Indulging yourself every now and then is fine but make sure that you keep within the limits you have to make sure you don't ruin your diet.

Chapter 5: 7 Day Meal Plan

When it comes to trying out new diets, most people often end up stumped after the first day or two. Why? This is because making meals while following certain restrictions can be a little confusing, if not daunting if you're doing it for the first time. So, to help you get past that, here's a 7 day meal plan that should help you get a feel for the Leptin diet.

Remember, there should be at least 5 hours between every meal.

Day 1:

- 2 boiled eggs and whole wheat toast for breakfast.

- Heirloom Tomato Mozzarella Salad for lunch. You can have any soup you want along with it.
- Coconut rice and grilled shrimp for dinner.

Day 2:

- Your choice of a breakfast smoothie and an apple.
- Turkey burger for lunch.
- Your choice of salad for dinner.

Day 3:

- Quinoa Egg bake for breakfast.
- Chicken chili for lunch.
- You can opt to have leftovers of the egg bake for breakfast or enjoy a salad of your choice.

Day 4:

- Your choice of breakfast smoothie.
- Steak burrito for lunch.
- Pesto shrimp with quinoa and brussel sprouts for dinner.

Day 5:

- Egg frittata for breakfast.
- Chicken cutlets with cherry salsa for lunch.
- Crunchy kale salad for dinner.

Day 6:

- Your choice of breakfast smoothie and some fruit.
- Wild salmon with pepita and lime butter for lunch.
- Chicken kebabs for dinner.

Day 7:

- Low carb hotcakes for breakfast.
- Quinoa and lentil salad with fully loaded avocado for lunch.
- Poached salmon with mango salsa for dinner.

**Keep in mind that the menu can be switched around depending on the activity you'll be having for a certain day. The more active you are, the more fuel your body needs.

Conclusion

Thank you again for reading this book!

I hope this book was able to help you to better understand what the Leptin diet is and how it can help you on your way to achieving better health as well as a fitter body.

The next step is to try out the different techniques and recipes we've provided in the book. After all, this is the only way through which you'll be able to tell if the diet is for you or not. Once more, thank you and happy dieting!

Finally, if you enjoyed this book, then I'd like to ask you for a favor, would you be kind enough to leave a review for this book on Amazon? It'd be greatly appreciated!

Thank you and good luck!

Keep reading for a free preview of my book:

"Ketogenic Diet Cookbook: The Belly Fat Burnin' Recipe Book for Losing Weight FAST with the Ketogenic Diet"!

Chapter 2 - Ketogenic Diet and Weight Loss

The key to successfully applying the ketogenic diet for any budget and personality is by planning ahead. People tend to give up more easily if they do not have a clear set of guidelines to follow. Weight loss, for instance, requires a high amount of willpower.

To begin the keto diet specifically for weight loss, here is a breakdown of the guidelines that you should always keep in mind:

Get rid of all the blatant carbohydrates that you have at home. Donate your breads, cookies, wheat pasta, and other such items to the nearest soup kitchen. Do not even glance at any shop that sells carbohydrates. The following should be banned from your plate (or eaten sparingly, that is to say, a tablespoon per month, maybe) bread, sweets, cereals, potatoes, legumes, beans, and sweet fruit.

Always keep a list of the following food items in your pocket: leafy green vegetables, meats (preferably lean and organic), including beef, fish and other seafood, eggs, chicken, pork, etc., healthy oils and fat (grass-fed butter, coconut, olive, macadamia), cheeses, protein shakes, and nuts. These are the foods that should always be on your plate to provide you with nutrients and energy.

Change your mindset from carb craving to fat and vegetable craving. For example, instead of bread sticks, think of celery sticks; instead of a bagel, try a pork bagel (the recipe is in the next chapter). While many vegetables still have carbohydrates in them, they also contain more fiber and nutrients than any carb-loaded dish out there.

Slowly, but surely, engage in regular workout sessions. Sign up at the gym and have someone guide you from low to high intensity interval workouts. You need to burn off those fat stores as efficiently as you can. Ask about weight training and cardio workouts to boost your metabolism.

Brace yourself for several days (or even weeks) of headaches, nausea, and other symptoms that have to do with the changes that your body is experiencing because of the diet. To prepare for this, make sure to replenish your electrolyte stores. Specifically, these are potassium, sodium and magnesium; these are some of the minerals that your body needs to function properly.

Make sure to read studies and reports about the keto diet so that you can adjust accordingly. Find a reliable online community on the keto diet to share information and meal plans with.

One final tip that you should never forget is to drink plenty of water every day. In a keto diet, you are going to be releasing stored water in your body. You want to catch up with that to avoid dehydration, so make sure to drink lots of water along with electrolytes.

Visit the link below using a computer to check out the rest of *"Ketogenic Diet Cookbook: The Belly Fat Burnin' Recipe Book for Losing Weight FAST with the Ketogenic Diet"*: http://www.books4everyone.com/ketogenic

Manufactured by Amazon.ca
Bolton, ON